BACKHOES

First edition.

Dan Osier

PowerKiDS press.

New York

Published in 2014 by The Rosen Publishing Group, Inc.
29 East 21st Street, New York, NY 10010

First Edition

Editor: Amelie von Zumbusch
Book Design: Andrew Povolny

Photo Credits: Cover iStockphoto/Thinkstock; p. 5 pryzmat/shutterstock.com; pp. 7, 13, 17, 21, 23 Dmitry Kalinovsky/shutterstock.com; p. 9 Hemera/Thinkstock; p. 11 Photodisc/Thinkstock; p, 15 a-poselenov/shutterstock.com; p. 19 Joseph Nettis/Photo Researchers/Getty Images.

Library of Congress Cataloging-in-Publication Data

Osier, Dan.
  Backhoes / by Dan Osier. — First edition.
    pages cm. — (Construction site)
  Includes index.
  ISBN 978-1-4777-2860-4 (library binding) — ISBN 978-1-4777-2953-3 (paperback) —
ISBN 978-1-4777-3030-0 (6-pack)
  1. Backhoes—Juvenile literature. I. Title.
  TA735.O85 2014
  629.225—dc23
                                        2013018990

Manufactured in the United States of America

CPSIA Compliance Information: W14PK3: For Further Information contact Rosen Publishing, New York, New York at 1-800-237-9932

Contents

Backhoes are useful. People dig and move dirt with them.

The word "backhoe" is short for "backhoe loader."

Backhoes got their name because they draw dirt back toward themselves.

The first ones were made in England.

The loader is in the front. It is used to carry things.

The bucket is used for digging. It is in the back.

The **stick** and **boom** connect the bucket to the tractor.

The **operator** sits in the tractor's cab.

SME-3419

19

Most backhoe operators work for construction companies. Others work for towns or on farms.

21

It is fun to watch a backhoe at work. Have you ever seen one?

WORDS TO KNOW

boom

operator

stick

WEBSITES

Due to the changing nature of Internet links, PowerKids Press has developed an online list of websites related to the subject of this book. This site is updated regularly. Please use this link to access the list: www.powerkidslinks.com/cs/backho/

INDEX